TREVOR LAWRENCE

NFL STAR

By Douglas Lynne

Book design by Jake Nordby
Cover design by Jake Nordby

Photographs ©: Matt Patterson/AP Images, cover, 1; Tom DiPace/AP Images, 4, 16, 23; David Rosenblum/Icon Sportswire, 6–7; Phelan M. Ebenhack/AP Images, 9; Hyosub Shin/Atlanta Journal-Constitution/AP Images, 10; John Byrum/Icon Sportswire, 12; Scott Strazzante/San Francisco Chronicle/AP Images, 15; Michael Owens/AP Images, 18; Kevin Sabitus/AP Images, 21; Red Line Editorial, 22

Press Box Books, an imprint of Press Room Editions.

Library of Congress Control Number: 2023909336

ISBN
978-1-63494-759-6 (library bound)
978-1-63494-766-4 (paperback)
978-1-63494-779-4 (epub)
978-1-63494-773-2 (hosted ebook)

Distributed by North Star Editions, Inc.
2297 Waters Drive
Mendota Heights, MN 55120
www.northstareditions.com

Printed in the United States of America
102023

ABOUT THE AUTHOR

Douglas Lynne is a freelance writer. He spent many years working in the media, first in newspapers and later for online organizations, covering everything from breaking news to politics to entertainment to sports. He lives in Minneapolis, Minnesota.

TABLE OF CONTENTS

TIME TO SHINE

1

Trevor Lawrence took the snap, dropped back, and was sacked. Things kept getting worse for the Jacksonville Jaguars. The team had picked Lawrence first in the 2021 National Football League (NFL) Draft. Most experts viewed the quarterback as a sure-thing star. But midway through his second year, he had yet to show it.

Trevor Lawrence prepares to throw a pass in a 2022 game against the Baltimore Ravens.

Lawrence scans the field for an open receiver.

The Jaguars started the 2022 season 3-7. Now they trailed the Baltimore Ravens 27-20. After the sack, only 1:51 remained in the

game. The Jags needed to go 86 yards for a touchdown. Jacksonville faced third and 21.

Nothing was going to rattle Lawrence on this sunny Florida afternoon. The 6-foot-6 quarterback completed a 16-yard pass. Then, on fourth down, he threw for 10 more yards. The Jaguars were on their way.

Soon they moved to the 10-yard line. Only 20 seconds remained. Lawrence fired the ball into the corner. Receiver Marvin Jones snagged it for a touchdown.

An extra point would have tied the game. Instead, the Jags put the ball back in Lawrence's hands. He delivered with another perfect throw for two points.

BIG THROWS

Trevor Lawrence completed 15 of 19 passes for 173 yards and 2 touchdowns in the fourth quarter. Two of those completions came on fourth down. He helped his team score 18 points in the final quarter and sparked a come-from-behind win.

Lawrence's clutch fourth-quarter performance secured a 28–27 win. Finally, he was playing like a franchise quarterback. He was only getting started.

 Lawrence celebrates with wide receiver Marvin Jones after throwing a touchdown pass to him.

2

CLEMSON KING

Trevor Lawrence was born on October 6, 1999, in Knoxville, Tennessee. However, he grew up in Cartersville, Georgia, a small city near Atlanta. By middle school, Trevor was turning heads as a quarterback. His football instincts were spectacular. Plus, he was already 6-foot-2.

Trevor became a superstar at Cartersville High School. He set

Trevor Lawrence led his high school football team to two Georgia state championships.

Lawrence posted a 38-2 record as a quarterback at Clemson University.

Georgia state records for passing yards and touchdowns. In 54 starts, he won 52 games. Strangers lined up for autographs. More than 100 college coaches came to watch him play. Experts considered Trevor the country's top high school player. Many expected him to choose the University of Georgia. It was just 100 miles from where he lived. Instead, Trevor decided to play for Clemson University in South Carolina.

Clemson was a big-time program when Lawrence arrived in 2018. The Tigers had been national champions two years earlier. And they had a good starting quarterback in Kelly Bryant. At first, Bryant and Lawrence shared time at quarterback. But after four games, Lawrence took over as the starter. Clemson was already 4-0. Under Lawrence, the team only got better. He could beat defenses by passing or running. Clemson kept on winning.

The Tigers met Alabama for the national title. Both teams were undefeated. Some

PB&J TIME

Trevor Lawrence had been skinny all his life. He wanted to gain weight to get stronger, but nothing seemed to work. After his freshman season, he figured it out. Eating lots of peanut butter and jelly sandwiches did the trick.

experts called Alabama's team the best in college football history. But after the game, everyone was talking about Lawrence. He threw for 347 yards and three touchdowns as Clemson dominated, 44–16. That performance capped one of the best freshman seasons in college football history.

Lawrence was even better as a sophomore. Once again, he led Clemson to an undefeated regular season. However, his team fell to Louisiana State University in the national title game.

Clemson was back in the playoff the next year too. This time they fell short of the title game. But Lawrence was runner-up for the Heisman Trophy, an award given to the best player in college football. Now he was ready for the NFL.

Lawrence passed for 10,098 yards in three years of college football.

A member of the Navajo Nation uses a pump to fill up a water drum in his truck.

role, too. The US government often ignores tribal rights.

The Navajo Water Project has ways to overcome these challenges. The group uses a community-led approach. By 2022, it had set up nearly 300 home water systems on the reservation. It also had set up more than 1,400 storage tanks.

NAVAJO WATER PROJECT

Emma Robbins is a Diné artist and activist. Diné people are also known as the Navajo. Robbins helps run the Navajo Water Project. This organization helps people get access to water. It often focuses on the Navajo Nation reservation. Robbins grew up there. At least 30 percent of homes on it have no running water. People use pumps or wells instead. But these often run dry. Many are **contaminated** by uranium. This metal came from old US government mines.

Robbins wanted to bring clean, safe water to her community. However, the problems were complex. People on the reservation often face poverty and lack of funding. **Racism** plays a may change the times when they move to new homes. In some cases, the new timing can kill them. It also harms people who rely on them for food. For example, some **Indigenous** peoples harvest corn, acorns, and salmon. If these foods disappear, people's health and traditions are impacted.

BIGGEST IMPACTS

Indigenous people tend to be most impacted by climate change. Tribal lands are often located in dry areas. In many cases, the US government forced people to move and stay there. Residents may have a hard time getting access to water. Droughts make this problem worse.

As more grasses spread to the Sonoran Desert and more wildfires burn in the region, saguaro cacti could die out.

Wildfires spread more easily in hot and dry weather. They can become bigger and more frequent. Large fires damage land and buildings. They also pollute the air with smoke.

Even the life cycles of plants and animals can change. Warmer weather can make flowers bloom earlier. Animals

The lighter areas of the rock show how much water levels in Lake Powell had dropped by April 2022.

When that happens, crops and animals can run out of water.

As temperatures rise, the ranges of plants and animals can shift. Some move to higher elevations. They may harm or crowd out other plants and animals. For example, bark beetles are killing trees throughout the Southwest.

Average temperatures in the Southwest are already rising. And scientists predict even warmer and drier conditions in the future. These changes increase chances of heat waves and droughts. They can also make these events last longer. Extreme heat can make people sick. It raises demand for water, too. As a result, shortages become more likely.

Higher temperatures also reduce the snowpack. That can lower water levels in rivers, lakes, and streams. These bodies of water depend on the melting snow. Some years might have less snow. Or the snow might melt earlier. Then water in reservoirs can run low or dry up.

CHAPTER 3

MANY IMPACTS

Climate change is affecting the Southwest. Aridification is one major threat. Many plants and animals are already at the high end of how much drought they can withstand. Even small changes can make it hard for them to survive. In the 2000s, for example, many piñon pine trees in New Mexico died.

These photos show the drying out of a New Mexico piñon forest between 2002 (left) and 2004 (right).

FRANCHISE QB

NFL fans had been eyeing Trevor Lawrence since his freshman year at Clemson. Many believed he had the tools to be an all-time great pro quarterback. In 2021, he finally got a chance to prove it. The Jacksonville Jaguars selected him with the first pick in the NFL Draft.

The Jaguars were coming off a miserable 1–15 season in 2020. Their fortunes didn't improve much in 2021.

Lawrence can beat defenses by passing and by running with the football for big gains.

Lawrence dives over defenders and reaches out to score a touchdown against the New York Jets.

Under first-year coach Urban Meyer, the Jaguars were a mess. Lawrence threw a league-high 17 interceptions compared to just 12 touchdowns. The team finished 3–14.

A new coach, Doug Pederson, took over in 2022. But the Jaguars continued to struggle, starting 3–7. However, fans began to notice changes in Lawrence. Pressure from defenses didn't seem to bother him as much. He was completing more of his passes and throwing fewer interceptions. Then he led the comeback win against the Baltimore Ravens. Suddenly the

THANK YOU, JACKSONVILLE

Trevor Lawrence and Marissa Mowry married in April 2021. The NFL Draft took place soon after. Jaguars fans expected their team to select Lawrence. So they purchased the couple a toaster as a wedding gift. Then they raised $11,000 for charities of the couple's choice. As a thank-you, the newlyweds donated $20,000 to local charities.

Jaguars were red hot. A 6–1 finish to the season put them in the playoffs.

The playoffs began terribly. Lawrence threw four first-half interceptions. Jacksonville trailed the Los Angeles Chargers 27–0. Lawrence said it was the worst half he'd ever played. Then he played what might have been his best half.

Lawrence began zipping passes all over the field. Instead of throwing interceptions, he threw touchdowns. Beginning late in the second quarter, he led four straight touchdown drives. A field goal on the last play of the game secured an amazing 31–30 comeback win. Lawrence had arrived. The future in Jacksonville had never looked brighter.

TREVOR LAWRENCE
CAREER PASSING STATISTICS
- **2021** – 3,641 yards, 12 TDs, 17 interceptions
- **2022** – 4,113 yards, 25 TDs, 8 interceptions

Lawrence celebrates after leading his team to victory in the playoffs.

TIMELINE MAP

1. **Knoxville, Tennessee: 1999**
   Trevor Lawrence is born on October 6.

2. **Cartersville, Georgia: 2017**
   Lawrence wraps up his prep career at Cartersville High School, where he set multiple state records.

3. **Clemson, South Carolina: 2018**
   Lawrence takes over as Clemson's starter in the fifth game of his freshman season. The Tigers defeat Syracuse 27-23 on September 29.

4. **Santa Clara, California: 2019**
   Lawrence leads Clemson to a 44-16 win over Alabama on January 7 to claim the national title.

5. **New Orleans, Louisiana: 2020**
   Lawrence and Clemson fall to Louisiana State in the national title game on January 13.

6. **Cleveland, Ohio: 2021**
   On April 29, the Jacksonville Jaguars select Lawrence with the first overall pick in the NFL Draft.

7. **Jacksonville, Florida: 2021**
   After losing his first five starts, Lawrence wins his first NFL game when the Jaguars beat the Miami Dolphins 23-20.

8. **Jacksonville, Florida: 2023**
   Lawrence leads the Jaguars to a 31-30 playoff victory over the Los Angeles Chargers after trailing 27-0 in the first half.

CHAPTER 4

SOLUTIONS

Many ways to fight climate change exist. Renewable energy is a major one. Renewable sources include wind and sunlight. They produce power without releasing greenhouse gas emissions.

The Southwest has many sunny days. For this reason, solar power is a good option. By the early 2020s, Utah and

Solar panels produce electricity in the Sonoran Desert in Arizona.

Arizona were leading states in solar power.

Distributed solar energy systems are also useful. These systems do not use large power plants. Instead, they produce power near where it will be used. Colorado has programs for this type of power. The programs help people put solar panels on the roofs of their homes. People can sell any extra electricity to power companies.

These efforts can slow climate change. But they won't stop it completely. People must adapt to changing conditions.

Conserving water is important. Individuals can work to use less water

A worker installs a solar panel on a roof in Denver, Colorado.

in their homes and yards. But bigger changes are also needed.

For example, agriculture uses most of the Southwest's water. Many ranchers in the area raise cattle. Cows eat crops such as hay and alfalfa. These crops use large amounts of water.

Scientists point to a few possible solutions. One is raising fewer cattle.

Then farmers can grow fewer crops. Instead, they can practice fallowing. They would skip planting crops for at least one season. The land then needs less water. Government programs can support this practice. States can pay farmers to fallow. That way, farmers won't lose money.

In addition to water, addressing wildfires is important. One method is controlled burns. These fires help lower the risk of large wildfires. This practice was once common. Indigenous peoples used controlled burns for thousands of years. But the US government stopped these burns in the 1900s. That change helped increase wildfires. Controlled

A farm growing wheat in Colorado is fallowing part of its fields.

burns started coming back in the late 1900s. Many tribes helped lead this effort.

Other changes focus on protecting vulnerable groups. Children, the elderly, and low-income people tend to be most at risk. These groups face greater health risks from heat waves and pollution. But they often have fewer ways to deal with them. They may also have trouble getting enough food or water. Cities across the Southwest are working to help. Many cities have set up food banks and community gardens. They help people get the resources they need to stay safe and healthy.

PHOENIX FIGHTS THE HEAT

Phoenix, Arizona, is the hottest major US city. In 2010, the city started a new project. It aimed to plant thousands of trees across Phoenix. But by 2021, little progress had been made. Meanwhile, heat-related deaths in Phoenix kept rising. That year, the city created a new department to focus on heat. One team helped unhoused people reach cooling centers. Another mission focused on trees and shade.

Unhoused people stay in a cooling center in Phoenix, Arizona, during a 2022 heat wave.

Where people live can put them at risk, too. Buildings in large cities trap heat. They create extra-hot areas known as urban heat islands. To protect people who live in these places, cities can plant trees. The trees' shade keeps areas cooler.

The Southwest is facing a serious climate crisis. But more and more people are working to help.

FOCUS ON
THE SOUTHWEST

Write your answers on a separate piece of paper.

1. Write a paragraph summarizing some of the harmful effects that climate change is creating in the Southwest.

2. Water can be scarce in the Southwest. In the area where you live, what resource is most important to protect or conserve? Why?

3. Which part of the Southwest has the lowest elevation?

    A. the deserts in the south
    B. the Rocky Mountains
    C. the plateaus in the north

4. Which period in the Southwest's history was the hottest and driest?

    A. 1000 to 1450
    B. 1905 to 1930
    C. 2000 to 2020

Answer key on page 32.